Alexander Eriksröd

Crude Oil as a Strategic Power Factor in International Relations

Examining the example Norway and the Conflict of National Interests in the Arctic

GRIN Verlag

Bibliografische Information der Deutschen Nationalbibliothek:

Die Deutsche Bibliothek verzeichnet diese Publikation in der Deutschen National-
bibliografie; detaillierte bibliografische Daten sind im Internet über http://dnb.d-
nb.de/ abrufbar.

Imprint:

Copyright © 2013 GRIN Verlag GmbH
Druck und Bindung: Books on Demand GmbH, Norderstedt Germany
ISBN: 978-3-656-41883-2

This book at GRIN:

http://www.grin.com/en/e-book/213323/crude-oil-as-a-strategic-power-factor-in-
international-relations

GRIN - Your knowledge has value

Der GRIN Verlag publiziert seit 1998 wissenschaftliche Arbeiten von Studenten, Hochschullehrern und anderen Akademikern als eBook und gedrucktes Buch. Die Verlagswebsite www.grin.com ist die ideale Plattform zur Veröffentlichung von Hausarbeiten, Abschlussarbeiten, wissenschaftlichen Aufsätzen, Dissertationen und Fachbüchern.

Visit us on the internet:

http://www.grin.com/

http://www.facebook.com/grincom

http://www.twitter.com/grin_com

CRUDE OIL AS A STRATEGIC POWER FACTOR IN INTERNATIONAL RELATIONS

EXAMINING THE

EXAMPLE NORWAY

AND THE

CONFLICT OF NATIONAL INTERESTS IN THE ARCTIC

Alexander M. Eriksroed

5BIK, 2012/13

International Business College Hetzendorf

Hetzendorferstraße 56-58, 1120 Wien

TABLE OF CONTENTS

PREFACE

I have now pondered writing a research paper about oil for a long time. Influenced by my father, who is Norwegian, my frequent visits to the country and a wish to study International Relations (IR) after graduation, this opportunity fits me surprisingly well.

That said, the main aim of this paper is to examine the role of oil in international politics, both by discussing past events related to it and by attempting to estimate its future role. The focus is not on exploring oil from a natural science point of view, but on examining which geopolitical roles oil plays when it comes to issues such as national security and the international balance of power.

INTRODUCTION

This academic research paper sets out to examine the role of oil in international politics. It will first be studied which importance oil carries as a commodity and power factor. Examples for the use of oil in international relations are given to illustrate the more theoretical backgrounds.

This paper employs two main examples: Norway, as an example of an oil-rich country and net exporter, and the Arctic region as an area of possible future conflict over oil. Using these examples, the different national interests will be shown to demonstrate what is at stake for the national states as well as for the international community.

It should be known to the reader that this paper, due to its limited extent, can only give a first impression of the topic. It is, nevertheless, a subject of universal relevance and, hopefully, interest.

Before examining why crude oil is so sought after this section will briefly display how crude oil is formed and processed. The many uses of crude oil in today's society will also be shown.

Crude oil was formed many million years ago from tiny plants and plankton below the surface of the sea. When plankton die, they descend to the bottom of the sea, adding to the layer of dead animals and plants one by one. The plankton is trapped under multiple layers of mud, sand and other sediments. As millions of years pass, these are buried deeper and deeper. Through the enormous heat and pressure exerted, they gradually turn the mud into rocks and the dead animals and plants into oil and gas.[1]

The ambition of this section is to show in how many varieties oil is used nowadays, often unnoticed.

- ❖ Fuels
  Petrol is a mixture of more than a hundred different hydrocarbons produced mainly through crude oil refining. Plane kerosene and diesel fall into the fuel category as well.
- ❖ Asphalt
  Used in road production, asphalt is based on crude oil. While, during the current economic decline, less asphalt is used for infrastructure projects, the consumption is expected to rise in the next years.[2]
- ❖ Heating
  Heating with gas is still common, despite the availability of more environmentally friendly solutions.
- ❖ Plastics
  Made up of polymers, plastics play an enormous role in our daily lives. This includes simple items such as plastic bags and boxes as well as consumer electric goods such as telephones, televisions and computers.
- ❖ Fertilizers
- ❖ Personal hygiene
  Perfume, soap, lip stick and hair spray are all made out of oil.
- ❖ Home interior
  Carpets, wallpapers, curtains and many other common objects are produced from crude oil.

The above list does not assert a claim to thoroughness, but is illustrates how dependent all of us have become on crude oil products.

---

[1] Der große Brockhaus in einem Band, "Erdöl", 2. Edition, Leipzig, 2005.
[2] Roadsbridges, "Asphalt consumption reboud", http://www.roadsbridges.com/north-america-leading-way-asphalt-consumption-rebound, (25.03.2013)

This section shall establish the role of oil in international relations; that is to say in international politics between states. It is first examined whether oil can be considered a strategic tool.

WHAT IS A STRATEGIC TOOL?

For the discussion in this research paper, a strategic tool shall be defined as every specific action taken by a legitimate government of a country with the intent to improve the position of the country relative to another country or countries. This can be action of economic, political, cultural, technological or societal nature. A strategic tool can, however, also come in the form of a resource, as described in the following.

EXAMPLES OF STRATEGIC TOOLS

Pertaining to oil, several strategic tools can be identified. What these tools have in common, is that they all fulfill the preconditions stated in the above paragraph.

Strategic oil stocks act as a palpable example. These are reserves of crude oil (and gas) hoarded by a country within its own borders. These reserves aim to guarantee the provision of fuel even if imports are halted. Such halts in import may be the result of transport failure or accident, but also of intentional non-delivery by petroleum-exporters.

Strategic oil stocks thus reduce the dependence on foreign suppliers, enabling the hoarding country to operate key government infrastructure in cases of emergency. The hoarding of strategic reserves can bring about very tangible benefits, as being able to endure oil export bans issued by other countries. As far as it is known, most governments retain a certain level of these reserves. According to the U.S. Department of Energy, the U.S. Strategic Petroleum Reserves stand at 727 million barrels, stored in underground salt domes in Texas and Louisiana. The reserves will be used in case of "severe energy supply interruption" and decided upon by the President.[3]

Other examples of strategic tools include weapons; especially weapons known to cause great suffering such as WMDs. Weapons of mass destruction comprise nuclear, biological and chemical weapons. Although international treaties for non-proliferation of these weapons are in place and every effort is made to have more countries sign and comply with these treaties, deterrence is still what has kept countries from using WMDs in the last decades. In other words, knowing that other countries dispose of these weapons has largely prevented their deployment. Although there have been exceptions, such as in Syria's civil war, when the Assad regime has allegedly used chemical weapons.[4] The odds are that in the future more countries will run WMD programs, according to Hans Blix.[5]

---

[3] U.S. Department of Energy, "Strategic Reserves Programme",
http://www.fossil.energy.gov/programs/reserves/spr/spr-facts.html, (25.03.2013)
[4] BusinessWeek, "Chemical weapons employed in Syria?", http://www.businessweek.com/news/2013-03-24/rogers-says-mounting-evidence-of-probable-chemical-weapon-use, (25.03.2013)
[5] Hans Blix, Chairman of the *Commission on Weapons of Mass Destruction* in a speech held on July 14, 2010 at the U.S. State Department in Washington D.C.

Because of countries' dependence on oil and the inability to "produce" oil (some countries will never be able to extract their own oil as it simply is not available in all areas) oil is, among others such as gas, but also wheat/grain and - to a certain extent - gold, a **strategic commodity**.

It might well be, that in the future, other commodities become of strategic importance. Examples include platinum, as it is used for the production of microchips which are used in almost all consumer technical goods.

Being a strategic commodity, oil might just be as important from a political view than from a production point of view. In some cases, merely knowing that "others" can dispose of it, can lead to conflicting desires and political insecurity.

The production of substantial amounts of crude oil is in the hands of relatively few states. Russia and Saudi-Arabia have led the list of crude oil producers for the last decades and will, most probably, do so in the years to come. According to CIA intelligence, Russia alone produced around 10.2 million barrels of crude oil per day in 2011. Other big players in the Middle and Far East include Kuwait, Iran, Iraq and the United Arab Emirates.[6]

Having established this, it becomes clear that the occurrence and accumulation of crude oil is very limited, geographically.

As the graph below shows, the biggest (confirmed) reserves are to be found in the Middle and Far East. The big circle placed on Canada indicates the reserves below the Arctic. These cannot (wholly) be attributed to Canada, however. The Arctic issue will be covered in the following.

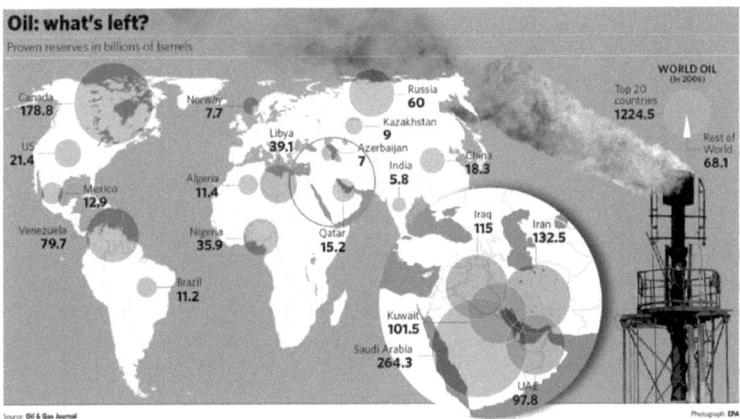

Source: http://www.sander.es/2012/01/world-oil-reserves/

It should be pointed out, that Central/Western Europe, despite hosting some of the countries with the highest consumption, does not hold substantial oil and gas reserves.

---

[6] Central Intelligence Agency, "The World Factbook", https://www.cia.gov/library/publications/the-world-factbook/rankorder/2241rank.html, (25.03.2013)

THE OPEC

This section shall examine the role and purpose of the Organization of Petroleum Exporting Countries (OPEC). It became clear to the author that rendering an account of the role of oil in today's society and international relations is not possible without mentioning the OPEC.

The Organization of Petroleum Exporting Countries currently has 12 members, namely Algeria, Angola, Ecuador, Iran, Iraq, Kuwait, Libya, Nigeria, Qatar, Saudi Arabia, the U.A.E. (United Arab Emirates) and Venezuela.[7] It provides a forum for the discussion of oil export policies and seeks to coordinate the efforts of its member countries. Any country with a "substantial net export of petroleum" may become a member of the OPEC. It is the declared aim of the OPEC to stabilize oil markets in order to secure an efficient, economic and regular supply of petroleum to consumers.[8]

This involves setting the price of the oil exported. Critics argue that the OPEC manipulates prices and sets them as high as possible in favor of the oil producing countries.

THE OPEC AND OIL IN INTERNATIONAL RELATIONS

Many OPEC members, including Saudi-Arabia, have long hoarded oil reserves, strictly controlling how much is sold on the world market. This proved very expensive for the exporting countries. Times of economic depression led to OPEC member countries releasing some of their reserves and flooding the market with oil. This, again, led to extreme fluctuations in prices.[9]

Between 2007 and 2008, the price per barrel rose from USD 50 to more than USD 140. By the end of 2008, it stood at a mere USD 30. Since then the price has continued to fluctuate heavily.[10] It can be argued that oil prices normally tend to extremes (highs or lows) considering that oil still is a must-have commodity for many with no substitute being available for it.

Hence it becomes clear that the OPEC has considerable influence on the international political stage. The ability to set prices for two-thirds of the oil produced globally carries significant weight.[11]

The remaining oil resources are concentrated in the Middle East to a great extent. The majority of OPEC member countries are Middle East countries.

Norway, the country used as an example of an oil-exporting country in this report, is not a member of the OPEC. According to the Norwegian government, becoming a member of the OEPC has never been a question, largely due to the conflict of interests that would occur considering that Norway is member of the IEA, the International Energy Agency. The IEA serves, according to Norwegian government officials, largely the interests of importing countries.

---

[7] OPEC, "About Us", http://www.opec.org/opec_web/en/about_us/25.htm, (03.04.2013)
[8] OPEC, "Our Members", http://www.opec.org/opec_web/en/about_us/23.htm, (03.04.2013)
[9] Foreign Affairs, "A crude predicament", http://www.foreignaffairs.com/articles/67890/robert-mcnally-and-michael-levi/a-crude-predicament#, (03.04.2013)
[10] Ibid.
[11] Norwegian government, "The oil market and Norway",
http://www.regjeringen.no/en/dep/oed/Subject/Oil-and-Gas/The-oil-market-and-Norway.html?id=461038, (03.04.2013)

In the following, it will be examined how Norway has in the past benefitted from its relatively vast oil resources and how these will influence future foreign policy of the Norwegian government.

RATIONALE FOR COUNTRY SELECTION

For the present research paper, Norway acts as an example of a country searching for, extracting, refining and exporting crude oil (and gas).

Norway was chosen because it is the first European country on the list of crude oil-producing countries. It ranks on place 15 with around 2 million barrels of crude oil produced per day in 2011.[12]

Norway is the world's second-biggest net exporter of gas and sixth-biggest net exporter of crude oil. The export of the two raw materials accounted for one third of all state revenues in 2008.[13] The estimated value of the remaining reserves lies at around 5,100 billion NOK (Norwegian crones).

Many Norwegian businesses operate in the oil and gas industry. STATOIL is the biggest Norwegian producer of oil and gas. Know-how plays an important role in the industry, with Norwegian businesses being world-leading when it comes to underwater drilling and drilling in the Antarctic.

NATIONAL OIL INDUSTRY OVERVIEW

With the discovery of "Ekofisk" crude oil reserves 300 kilometers south of the Norwegian border in 1969, the Norwegian petroleum industry began to flourish. In 1971, production at "Ekofisk" field began. This marked the beginning of years of many discoveries in the North Sea and along the long Norwegian coast.[14]

By 2009, more than NOK 3,000 billion had been invested in exploration and discovery of new oil fields only. In contrast, the sector had created more than double that value for Norway, around NOK 8,000 billion.[15]

It is expected that by now 35-40 % of the total reserves have been exploited. [16]

INFLUENCE ON FOREIGN POLICY

Norway has always had to rely on diplomacy and peaceful negotiations to achieve its goals on the world political stage. This is due to several reasons. Norway is a rather small country by

---

[12] Central Intelligence Agency, "The World Factbook",
https://www.cia.gov/library/publications/the-world-factbook/rankorder/2241rank.html, (25.03.2013)
[13] Norwegen in Österreich, "Wirtschaftszweige",
http://www.norwegen.or.at/About_Norway/business/Wirtschaftszweige/oilgas/, (25.03.2013)
[14] Norwegian government, "Oil history in five minutes",
http://www.regjeringen.no/en/dep/oed/Subject/Oil-and-Gas/norways-oil-history-in-5-minutes.html?id=440538, (26.03.2013)
[15] Ibid.
[16] Ibid.

population (five million inhabitants). Also, Norway is not a great military power. The Northern European country does not possess nuclear weapons.

Norway is neither a member of the European Union nor the Eurozone. The country is, however - through many treaties such as the European Free Trade Agreement (EFTA) - closely involved and integrated into the European community of states. This has enabled Norway to benefit greatly from economic cooperation without having to devote funds to common political goals. In two referendums (1972 and 1994) the Norwegian population rejected the wish of some of its politicians to apply for EU membership. It is, since then, custom practice in Norwegian politics not to bring up the topic again.

Norway has, over the years, become a popular location for international political events of dispute settlement and the passage of treaties. In 1993, the "Declaration of Principles on Interim Self-Government Arrangements" was signed in Oslo in an attempt to resolve the deadlocked Israeli-Palestinian conflict. Similarly, a treaty on the ban of land mines was signed in Oslo in 1997. Norway enjoys a reputation for being a neutral and safe ground for negotiations.

Oil may impinge on foreign policy in a myriad of decisive ways.

It is expected that, due to its scarcity, oil will play an increasingly important role in international relations and might well be used as a strategic factor in negotiations and trade disputes.

To be more specific, two types of uses of oil and gas in international relations can be identified.

1. **Oil as a treat**

   Today, the commerce with crude oil and gas is an important global industry. Countries that have a net excess of oil/gas, that is to say have remains left after covering their own needs (and allocating provisions for strategic reserves) sell oil to countries with which they maintain trade relations.

   Exporting countries are in the favorable position of being able to choose to whom they sell. This decision can be based on multiple factors. According to the market principle, oil will be sold to the country paying the highest price. Clearly, market distortions are common, leading to exporting countries choosing not to deliver to the highest bidder in some cases. This may be because the importing country is considered untrustworthy or would not employ the oil in a way agreeable to the exporter.

   Trading with oil can well be considered a treat in some cases, and as a way of showing trust in a country.

2. **Oil as a threat**
   Not starting or interrupting the trade with oil is a powerful device. When employed correctly, this hostile measure can bring about favorable results for exporter. For the importer, the repercussions of a total embargo (provided the country is dependent on a single supplier) can have catastrophic repercussions, however.

   As an example, the Russian natural gas monopolist Gazprom reduced Ukraine's supply of gas by a quarter in the winter of 2008. The dispute was over bills which, according to

Gazprom had not been paid.[17] In January 2009, Russia cut off the gas supply to Ukraine completely for thirteen days. As a result, many homeowners were unable to heat during one of the coldest periods of winter.[18]

As the following example illustrates, not only interrupting trade, but also actively forcing others to suspend their trade of oil is a feasible policy option in some parts of the world.

A third of the world's traded oil passes through the Strait of Hormuz, a narrow strip of water linking the Persian Gulf and the Arabian Sea. With a narrow part of only 33 km, closing the strategically important bottleneck is thinkable to interrupt ship transport. This is exactly what Iran has indirectly threatened to do repeatedly in the last years. In the last incident of January 2013, the Iranian envoy to Baghdad, Hassan Danaie-Far, left all options on the table for Iranian leadership.[19]

One can argue, however, that Iran would hurt itself more than any other country by closing the Strait of Hormuz. This is partly because Iran relies on oil export revenues for the biggest part of its economy and partly because China, one of the biggest importers of Iranian Oil is one of the few remaining countries on relatively friendly terms with the Islamic Republic.[20]

---

[17] BBC News, "A cold dispute", http://news.bbc.co.uk/2/hi/business/7274380.stm, (26.03.2013)
[18] „The Russo-Ukrainian Gas Dispute of January 2009: a comprehensive assessment",
http://www.oxfordenergy.org/wpcms/wp-content/uploads/2010/11/NG27-
TheRussoUkrainianGasDisputeofJanuary2009AComprehensiveAssessment-
JonathanSternSimonPiraniKatjaYafimava-2009.pdf, (26.03.2013)
[19] Israel National News, "Iran Warns of Strait of Hormuz Closure If US Chooses 'War'",
http://www.israelnationalnews.com/News/News.aspx/164555#.UViXTDtu5kI, (31.03.2013)
[20] Bloomberg, "Closing strait of Hormuz might be self-inflicted wound for Iran",
http://www.bloomberg.com/news/2011-12-28/closing-strait-of-hormuz-might-be-self-inflicted-wound-
for-iran.html, (31.03.2013)

LOCATION

The Arctic covers the vast area around the North Pole, which is mainly covered by ice. It extends for around 26 million sq km.

According to American scientists' estimates, the sea below the Arctic holds 13 % of the total crude oil as well as 30 % of all gas reserves still to be extracted. Substantial amounts of gold, coal and iron ore are also expected.[21]

As stated in the United Nations' convention on the Law of the Sea of 1982, the Arctic does not belong to any state in particular, but to "the whole of humanity". Specifically, the convention, ratified by all parties involved (see next section), lays out the rights of bordering states and the exact location of sea lanes and transport routes for air transport.[22]

According to the United Nations' convention on the Law of the Sea (UNCLOS), every country has the sole right to the area extending 370 km from its coastal line.

The convention states, for instance, the right of "innocent passage" for ships of all States, but also prohibited actions, such as testing weapons of any kind, threatening sovereignty of the Coastal States, fishing activities, mining, any resource-extracting, and polluting of the environmentally sensitive area.

CONFLICT & PARTIES INVOLVED

Five riparian states of the Arctic can be identified: the United States, Canada, Russia, Norway and Denmark. Note that Denmark represents Greenland when it comes to questions of foreign policy.

The clearer it becomes that all currently known reserves of oil and gas will be depleted within several decades (at the most), the more neighboring states attempt to prove that their territory extends further than currently known. This, by extension, grants the countries the full and only right to all oil and gas reserves and mineral resources.

For decades, nations have not asserted claims on Arctic territory for such obvious reasons as remoteness and inhospitability. This is about to change.

In 2007, Russia planted its flag on the seabed (4,200 m deep) below the Arctic. In what seemed like an act of defiance to many, this action furthered Moscow's' claims to the Arctic. After it became public that Russia had planted a titanium flag below the Arctic, reactions ranged from indignation to anger. The Canadian prime minister argued that "this isn't the 15th century" and "you can't go around the world and just plant flags and say 'We're claiming this territory'".

---

[21] Die Welt, "Start frei für Run auf die Arktis",
http://www.welt.de/wissenschaft/umwelt/article8900622/Start-frei-fuer-den-Run-auf-die-Schaetze-der-Arktis.html, (31.03.2013)
[22] United Nations, "UNCLOS",
http://www.un.org/Depts/los/convention_agreements/texts/unclos/closindx.htm, (31.03.2013)

Norwegian government has, in the last years, made the Arctic and the High North its number one foreign policy priority. "Regjeringens nordområdestrategi", the governments "High North strategy", lays out the strategic interests and claims the Norwegian government puts forth.

The strategic paper, known to the public since December 2006, puts a focus on scientific research and becoming a leader in knowledge about the High North area.[23]

When it comes to resources, the paper presents a focus on sustainable petroleum development and consideration of "several new developments".

In a separate chapter, the importance of Norwegian-Russian relations is described. Norway considers it vital to "maintain close bilateral relations with Russia", which is both a neighbor and the country with which Norway shares the Barents Sea. The paper states that a number of challenges in the High North, especially in the field of resource management, can only be solved with Russia's engagement and Norwegian-Russian cooperation. In general, Norwegian governments' policy towards Russia is based on "pragmatism, interests and cooperation."[24]

As far as active steps are concerned, the High North strategy states that Norway "will further develop petroleum activities in the Barents Sea area through an active licensing policy that takes into account the need to follow up exploration results and the need to open up new areas for exploration."

When studying the developments in Norwegian foreign policy with regards to the Arctic, several interesting aspects can be identified. The Norwegian government

> Recognizes that energy aspects become the focus of attention and acquire a foreign policy dimension in the Arctic.
> Concedes that economic interests play an increasing role in questions relating to the High North.
> Is well aware that the potential for conflicts in the High North is increasing.
> Aims to shift the focus from avoiding talks about conflict to openly addressing these issues.
> Acknowledges that different views exist on the exact location of delimitation lines.
> Acknowledges that the issue of delimitation of the Continental shelf can only be resolved through political agreement between Norway and Russia.

KEY REASONS FOR EXPLOITING HIGH NORTH PETROLEUM RESERVES

1) Economic interests

Two factors that are closely connected make extracting petroleum increasingly interesting and highly rewarding. Firstly, the rising price for petroleum, leading to higher revenues per barrel. Secondly, the decreasing level of reserves, combined with increasing demand, resulting in even higher prices.

---

[23] The High North Strategy, page 8, (02.04.2013)
[24] The High North Strategy, page 9, (02.04.2013)

2) Political interests

Norway aims to be able to provide all petroleum it needs within its borders and not having to rely on imports. Considering this goal as well as the fact that reserves diminish at a constant rate, new sources have to be located.

This also enables Norway to maintain its current level of petroleum exports and export revenues. It is likely that the Norwegian governments' power in negotiations and political independence will only increase following these developments.

POSSIBLE SCENARIOS

The majority of countries staking claims to the resources of the Arctic have so far done so unofficially only. Norway and Russia are the only countries to have officially filed such a claim.[25]

Several future scenarios for the management of resource-extraction are thinkable.

It is without doubt that one can postulate that, in the next two to three decades, serious efforts will be undertaken in the Arctic region to extract crude oil. It is not clear, however, whether these efforts will be made based on cooperation and mutual benefit, as the five riparian states all assure the public today.

In the following, two distinct scenarios shall be drawn up. The first one, rather optimistic, relies on the international community overcoming their differences and cooperating. The second one, rather more pessimistic – and more realistic, as some might argue – is based on hostility and "survival of the fittest"-mentality.

The author would like to add, that the two models shown merely represent the outermost positions of a continuum and many other combinations and gradations are possible.

OPTIMISTIC SCENARIO (1)

As oil and gas reserves continue to decline, the international community of states reaches consensus to set up an international treaty that is ratified and respected by all states. It regulates who has the right to extract the remaining resources in the High North area. This is done without major incidents. The following paragraphs describe how such an accord could, if at all, be reached.

The first step would most probably consist of an international treaty being drawn up. Any state, whether a High North country or not, beginning to extract Arctic resources on a large scale without backing by such an international agreement would draw the anger of the international community of states. It is not unthinkable that, if a state were to do so nevertheless, retaliation and political sanctions would be the consequence.

A treaty on the extraction of Arctic resources would, in any case, most likely favor the neighboring states, being the United States, Canada, Russia, Norway and Denmark. But how may the distribution between these states look like?

---

[25] National Security Law, "Canada wants guns on Canadian boats heading to the arctic", http://nationalsecuritylawbrief.com/2010/10/24/conservative-party-in-canada-wants-guns-on-canadian-boats-heading-to-the-arctic/, (02.04.2013)

As of today, it can be speculated that the United States and Russia, due to their sheer size, population and political influence would enjoy some kind of privilege. Norway and Denmark, being the smallest states by far, might well come off worst. On the other hand, Norway has already officially filed a claim to the Arctic resources.

One could also argue that Russia, disposing of large oil and gas reserves within its borders, does not need to gain access to Arctic resources.

All speculations aside, it becomes very clear that even if Arctic oil and gas reserves are extracted in well-ordered circumstances, they will not at all satisfy current consumption, not even speaking of a level of consumption higher than todays'. Having said this, part of this scenario might include/will have to include a drastic change in overall energy politics and consumption habits, stretching well beyond efficiency increases and minor energy sector reforms as they can be observed today.

At present, such a positive development seems rather unlikely considering the enormous conflict of interests. It may well be, that the future develops in a way resembling scenario number two, described in the following.

PESSIMISTIC SCENARIO (2)

The increasing accessibility of Arctic resources along with the growing military presence of circumpolar states is a recipe for competition and potential conflict.

This scenario will be the likely result of 1) a state beginning to extract Arctic resources without the approval of the state community or 2) inability of the state community to conclude an agreement regulating resource management in the High North.

The issue of resource management in the Arctic is not a new one and has long been on the agenda. Due to the problems' complexity, seeming insolubility and the presence of other more pressing issues, however, it has often been pushed into the background. Until today.

In this paper, it has been described extensively how enormous an importance oil has in society. This is why the situation in the Arctic, partly already tense today, could easily get out of control; with state leaders resorting to the most extreme measures to meet their nations' energy needs.

The main challenge for the Arctic states is that states such as China, India, South Korea but also the European Union will regard the Arctic sea as international territory just like any other sea, according to a report entitled "Climate Change & International Security: The Arctic as a Bellwether", published in 2012.

As an example, former Russian president and now-prime minister Dmitry Medvedev stated in 2008 that "our [Russia's, ed.) first and main task is to turn the Arctic into Russia's resource base of the 21st century."[26] The fact that Medvedev publicly issued such a statement speaks of the strategic importance of the area. In the last time it can be seen that the parties involved lay down their claims in shortening intervals. It is unprecedented to have numerous major policy

---

[26] The Kremlin, "Speeches and Press Releases",
http://archive.kremlin.ru/eng/text/speeches/2008/09/17/1945_type82912type82913_206564.shtml,
(08.04.2013)

announcements from so many major players in such a short timeframe.[27] One might draw from this the conclusion that the current saber-rattling may quickly turn into (armed) conflict.

Another interesting feature of this conflict is its ambiguity. Norway and Russia increase their military presence and rearm in the High North, while at the same time they sign a treaty regarding boundaries in the Barents Sea.[28] This indicates that the Arctic States touched by the issue share a common interest in quieting it down.

Getting to the point, the following part shall demonstrate how international disagreement and friction can lead to conflict.

It is important to know how a military conflict in the High North could be triggered. Only then it becomes clear how it can be avoided.

TURNING POINT

Utilizing the example Norway, the last part of this report examines the repercussions of Norway (hypothetically) starting to drill for oil in the Arctic areas that are currently not clearly assigned to one state's territory.

Norway, through its state-owned oil company Statoil, starts drilling for oil in the sea below the Arctic. This will, in any case constitute the first step, as installing pipelines and other infrastructure of high financial intensity will follow afterwards only.

Norway discovers an oil field. By now, all Arctic powers (besides other nations) are aware of the Norwegian involvement in the Arctic. Intelligence technology makes it possible to easily assess the difference between a small-scale research project and the extraction of oil.

In any case, this step would be followed by outcries of anger by other national governments; warnings and advice to halt the extraction process would pursue. If, by now, Norway does not refrain from extracting more crude, and publicly affirm this step, tensions might be rising at a considerable pace. From now on, every second that passes is crucial in the eyes of other world leaders. Obviously, all parties are aware that the oil in question can only be extracted once.

The reader must be aware, that from this point onwards, the assumptions made for scenario two become more and more uncertain.

It is probable that the community of states would quickly demand an explanation from the Norwegian government at high political level. What might follow is a request to halt the extraction process as long as negotiations are in progress. This, obviously, defeats the purpose of being the first country to start extraction, and Norway might ignore these. For anyone acquainted with Norwegian politics, this development seems difficult to imagine, but when it matters decisions made tend to become less rational.

It is exactly this irrationality of high-level political decision-making that poses the biggest threat hereafter. All it takes for armed conflict to break out is a combination of political insecurity and the urge to act on the domestic front, meaning the people of a country demanding immediate action by their political leader.

---

[27] Climate Change & International Security: The Arctic as a Bellwether, "Executive Summary", http://www.c2es.org/publications/climate-change-international-arctic-security, (08.04.2013)
[28] The Guardian, "Military rivalry in the Arctic", http://www.guardian.co.uk/world/2012/jun/05/arctic-military-rivalry-cold-war, (07.04.2013)

Russian government, not approving of the Norwegian policy move and increasingly under pressure to act from internally, deploys combat troops and install military capabilities in the High North. This has already been happening, according to several news reports.[29] Nuclear submarines (especially of the United States) patrol the High North area constantly.

As energy prices keep rising and internal pressure is put on Russian leadership, after years of difficulty of supplying reasonably priced oil, the point of no return is reached.

Russia attacks the Norwegian oil extraction installations and seizes control of the compound. Having prepared this step for months and using considerable force, the attack is a swift one.

Following the Norwegian governments' political outcry, the international community of states might warn Russia to step back. Another factor of involvement is Norwegian membership in the North American Treaty Organization (NATO). Theoretically, other NATO members are obliged to defend any member country under attack. Other NATO members include the United States, the United Kingdom and Germany.

What the consequence of military involvement of one of these states in the Arctic would be is not imaginable. In terms of human suffering (let alone the environmental damage to one of the most pristine areas of the world) one would rather not think about the dire effects of major military powers battling in the Arctic.

---

[29] "World's armies circle as Arctic warms to reveal untapped supplies of oil and gas", http://worldnews.nbcnews.com/_news/2012/04/16/11222215-worlds-armies-circle-as-arctic-warms-to-reveal-untapped-supplies-of-oil-and-gas?lite, (08.04.2013)

Concluding, it can be said that oil, as a strategic commodity, is of incredible importance to nations around the world. Knowing that the world's reserves diminish at an incredible rate while consumption levels rise steadily, it becomes clear that oil will increasingly be used as a strategic tool and as a means of reaching national objectives.

Apart from the Middle East, vast reserves of oil and gas are expected below the Arctic. As polar ice melts away as a result of climate change, these reserves are uncovered and national interests to tap them will collide more and more.

If cooperative political mechanisms cannot keep pace with developments in the Arctic region, competition and conflict will be the likely result.

As a first step, the Arctic states should reconsider their prohibition on the discussion of issues of military security.

Secondly, forms of peaceful cooperation need strengthening, as has been done successfully in fields such as "search and rescue". Organizations such as the Arctic Council must provide a platform for the discussion of national security needs before they get out of hand and it is too late for diplomatic resolution.

It remains to be seen whether the international community of states manages to overcome its differences of opinion and increases cooperation to extract the last resources left on our planet.

If not, only a grim picture of the future of energy supply can be painted. It is a picture of war, human suffering and ecocide.